Wildflowers
For Wildlife

Plants To Make Your Garden
Wildlife Friendly

by

Jenny Steel

Osmia **Publications, Banbury**

First published in 2001 by *Osmia* Publications, Banbury

ISBN 0-9539906-2-1

Cover Photograph: Jenny Steel and Alan Pottinger

Production by *Osmia* Publications

Designed by Louisa Stevens

Printed and bound in Thailand by Gift Export Co. Ltd

Acknowledgements

I would like to thank several people for helping with the preparation of this book. Rose O'Toole provided support and enthusiasm for the project and Chris O'Toole used his editing skills to great effect. Stanley Woodell and Chris O'Toole both contributed some additional information. I would also like to thank Louisa Stevens who used her considerable skills in designing the book and Larry Snell for all his hard work.

Lastly my special thanks must go to my husband Alan Pottinger for reading the first draft of the book, for his skilful photography, but mostly for his endless support and encouragement.

Dedication

This book is dedicated to my mother and father, who showed me the joys of gardening and the beauty of the countryside.

About the Author

Jenny Steel carried out plant ecology research at Oxford University before establishing and running her own wildflower plant nursery. For the last 10 years she has devoted much of her time to writing, broadcasting and teaching courses on wildlife gardening. In 1999 she helped Alan Titchmarsh make a wildflower meadow on BBC2's Gardener's World and presented a series of wildlife gardening items on BBC2's How Does Your Garden Grow. She is a frequent broadcaster on BBC Radio Oxford.

Her 2 acre garden near Oxford has featured in many magazine articles and is the venue for her one day courses on wildlife gardening. She also runs residential courses at adult education colleges around the country.

www.wildlife-gardening.co.uk

Contents

ONE

Why grow wildflowers?

Just about every town around the country has a garden centre or plant nursery nearby. For many of us, part of our weekend leisure time nowadays is taken up with visiting these wonderful places overflowing with the biggest, the newest, the most colourful flowers for planting in your garden. The selection of these varieties and cultivars increases year by year, as plant breeders work ever harder to produce attractive flowering plants for our garden borders. So why then should we want to include wildflowers in our gardens? Many of them have smaller flowers than the garden plants we are used to and they may well flower for shorter periods. Some can be invasive – seeding freely into any available space. Surely they are only appropriate for those 'lost' areas in the garden, maybe at the bottom of a hedge, or in the long grass at the end of the garden where nothing else will grow? This book will show you how useful and versatile our native plants are, and how to include them in even a tiny back yard.

Attracting wildlife

Many wildflowers are not only suitable for garden cultivation, but enhance the garden environment in ways that non-native plants may not. We should not neglect non native flowers entirely - there are many, especially cottage garden types with single flowers, which will attract a range of insects. But where wildlife is concerned those large, colourful blooms in the garden centre often have nothing to interest passing insects, as the flower parts that normally produce the pollen and nectar that insects require, have been replaced by extra petals. They may be attractive to us, but they certainly aren't to bees, butterflies and other pollinating insects.

Pollination

Flowering plants have bright, colourful and often scented blooms to attract insects and thus ensure that pollination is carried out. Bees are the most important pollinators: the majority of species of insect-pollinated plants are specialised for pollination by these insects. Bees are the best pollinators because they actively collect pollen as food for their larvae and they have evolved special structures on their bodies for handling and transporting pollen. Producing an excess of pollen, together with sweet nectar, is the price that plants pay in return for the pollination services provided by bees and other insects. Pollination occurs when pollen grains from the anthers, the male parts of the flower, are deposited onto the stigma, the female part. This allows the flower to be fertilised and develop seeds for reproduction. Some flowers, known as self-fertile, can self-pollinate when pollen from their own anthers falls on the stigma. However, the flowers of many plants cannot be fertilised by their own pollen - they are self-sterile and need to be fertilised by pollen from flowers of another plant of the same species.

Although bees are by far the most important pollinators, moths, butterflies, beetles, flies and wasps also pollinate some of our wildflowers by transferring pollen from one flower to another. All these insects are especially adapted to seek out and pollinate our native plants.

Luckily we have a vast number of native plants at our disposal, and planting a careful selection of these in our gardens is a fantastic way of supporting local wildlife and encouraging a wide range of bees, butterflies and many other attractive and useful insects. Also, some of our most colourful birds such as goldfinches and linnets find the food they need in the seeds of certain wildflowers and we can assist their survival while enjoying their company in our gardens, by planting species with nutritious seeds.

The many species of insect that visit native wildflowers do so to feed on the nectar and pollen the plants produce. On a wider scale, these insects are themselves food for a whole host of other creatures, from the reptiles and amphibians that may be around, to the smaller mammals like shrews, hedgehogs and bats. Thus, wildflowers will indirectly help not only these mammals but frogs, toads, grass snakes and slow worms to name a few. Also many of our native birds will visit a garden rich in insects for their food supply. Robins, wrens, tits, warblers, thrushes – there is a long list of bird species searching the countryside for insect food for themselves and their offspring. Some of these birds are just as happy in the garden environment as they are in fields and hedgerows, and will visit your garden eagerly if natural food is present. This interdependence of different creatures is the garden 'food chain' and by growing wildflowers you will be helping to keep the links in the chain connected.

Conservation

Although attracting wildlife to the garden is what this book is about, there are other very valid reasons for cultivating wildflowers. Firstly, many of our native plants are exceptionally beautiful –elegant, colourful, even dramatic in their own way. The common poppy is a good example of a flower with all three of these attributes, and highly suitable for garden cultivation. Although the poppy is declining in the wild, most of us have the opportunity to see this plant in its natural habitat – field margins, roadsides and cornfields. Its seed can lie dormant for a very long time and will burst into life when conditions are right for their germination. But for many of us, there is a long list of flowers we will now never see, as their natural habitats shrink and are lost. The figures relating to these habitat losses are well known, but by growing some of these lost rarities in our gardens we have the chance to see them and continue their propagation. There may come a time when gardeners are seen as custodians of such beauties as pasque flower or the snake's head fritillary.

The suitability of wildflowers for gardens

Not all native flowers are suitable for gardens. Some are very invasive, and best avoided even in a large garden. Hogweed is one of the best hoverfly attractants in the summer months, but it will soon take over the garden if given the chance! Coltsfoot is another very attractive plant, flowering early in the year when we are all in need of a breath of spring. However, it too spreads very rapidly, and planting it in your garden border is probably a mistake.

In conclusion, there are many wildflowers to add to your existing plant collection, all of which will greatly enhance the wildlife value of your area. This small book describes 30 such plants, divided into groups for different garden situations, some of which correspond to the natural habitats we are losing in the wild. All the plants have been chosen for their ability to adapt to a garden situation, their ease of propagation at home, and their attractiveness to the insects and birds visiting your garden.

TWO

Garden habitats

Every garden is different. Whether we are looking at the type of soil you have, the sunlight or shade, or the amount of space available, a huge number of variable factors operate. Add to these factors the trees and shrubs already there, your own preferences for flower colour or type of plant - even who will use your garden and for what, and you will soon see that no two gardens could ever be the same. And the closer you look at the conditions within your own garden the more you will become aware of the small differences between one spot and another. There may be dry shady places under trees or shrubs, bright sunny places where the soil never seems to dry out, or lots of traditional borders full of bright double petalled plants. This book will look at the different areas within your own garden, and give you some ideas for the best native wildflowers that will happily adapt to your conditions.

Bare in mind also that many wildflowers generally grow in poor, unfertilised soils in the wild. This means that in the garden they will flourish in places where other plants will not. If your soil is richer, wildflowers will still grow - they may however produce more leaves and fewer flowers than those grown in more nutrient hungry soils.

The concept of habitats in the garden can be confusing but once you start to look in more detail at these separate little places, under trees or around a pond, for instance, you will begin to appreciate these different spots, and see why some plants will enjoy your particular conditions, whilst others may not. In order to help you choose species suitable for these different areas in your garden, we will look, at the start of each section, at the natural habitats in which those wildflowers grow. The sections are:

Dry rocky places
Lightly shady spots
Grassy meadows
Damp places

A further chapter on wildflowers suitable for cultivation in traditional borders is also included.

It is worth remembering that our gardens don't correspond to any natural habitat anywhere in the world. One thing is certain - gardens as a whole are very unnatural places. They contain collections of plants that would not normally be found together, managed in an artificial way. Some of those plants will be exotic species from North America or China and of little value to our native wildlife. Others may be cultivated varieties of some of our own British plants, such as cornflowers or violets. What we need to do, as wildlife gardeners, is to weave this whole plant patchwork together in order to ensure that we are providing the food that our wildlife needs.

Gardening with nature

There is one very important consideration if you are hoping to attract more wildlife into your plot and that is to 'garden with nature'. This means trying to take into account your immediate surroundings and the natural conditions round about you. If you live in the middle of the city, it is unlikely, but not impossible, that the marbled white butterfly will visit you. Small tortoiseshell butterflies almost certainly will, so it is important to choose wildflowers like small scabious or wild marjoram, which will provide nectar for the small tortoiseshell.

Gardens are areas where a great deal of disturbance takes place. We are forever turning over the soil, pulling out weeds, mowing the lawn or spiking it to aerate the soil beneath. All this activity can disturb the wild creatures already in the garden, whether they be moth larvae beneath the soil or grasshoppers in long grass. How we manage and look after the garden is a crucial factor in looking after the wildlife there. Each habitat section of this book will give guidelines for the activities necessary to keep that part of the garden looking good, whilst protecting the wildlife that may live there.

THREE
Growing your own wildflowers from seed

Growing plants from seed is satisfying, economical and easy. Of course, we are all now aware that plants should never be taken from the wild but it can be difficult to find native species in garden centres and plant nurseries. By growing our own we can ensure that they are true natives, by using seeds guaranteed to be of native origin from a specialist supplier. This is a crucial point – we need to ensure that the plants we are growing are those that our native wildlife is used to. Although many of the species we are interested in also grow on the Continent, their genetic makeup may be slightly different from our own plants, and there is risk of contamination of our own genetic stock.

So how do we go about growing wildflowers from seed? Many of us have tried and failed, and are put off when seeds sown in trays of compost fail to germinate - we assume it is beyond our horticultural abilities. It certainly is not. But wildflower seeds come in all shapes and sizes, and to assist germination we need to know a little about them, and what happens to them in the wild in order to unlock their potential and allow them to spring into life.

Germination in the wild

After pollination, seed will set and fall to the ground, where hopefully it will find its way to the soil surface. This is no mean feat! The soil may be covered with other plants, particularly grasses, and if 'seed to soil' contact is not made the seed will not germinate. Some seeds will be eaten by birds or small mammals. Seeds are an important source of nourishment for these animals, but there will be many other hazards preventing germination. This helps to explain why some plants produce vast numbers of seeds. A single ox eye daisy plant may set many thousands of seeds, but only a very tiny percentage will germinate and grow.

Seeds of some species may germinate straight away if they find the soil surface. Plants that do this are generally referred to as autumn germinators, and they spend the winter as small plants or seedlings, waiting for warmer spring weather before they continue their growth. Some annuals, and corncockle is a good example, behave in this way – it gives them a head start when spring arrives. But the majority of wildflower seeds remain on the soil surface and wait until spring before germination occurs.

During the winter months, there are many forces at work on these seeds. There may be snow, frost, and heavy rain. The soil may be churned about by animals, birds, farm machinery or your garden fork. A great many of our wild plants have adapted to these huge changes in external conditions, and some species will not germinate without them. Once we know a little about these forces, we can put them to our advantage to ensure good germination of our wildflower seeds.

Vernalisation

Many plants require the cold conditions of winter before they will spring into life. This process is known as vernalisation. The action of frost breaks down the seed coat to allow water to enter and stimulate the process of growth. Often, it is not simply a question of needing below zero temperatures. The seed may need to be frozen, then warmed up, then frozen again. This may need to happen several times before dormancy is broken and of course this occurs naturally through our winters. It is hard to mimic these conditions, even by leaving seeds in the refrigerator or freezer which seed packets often suggest. For foolproof germination sow these seeds in the winter and leave them outside. Allow nature to do what she does best! In general any members of the Primula family (primrose, cowslip, oxlip), the Geranium family (the cranesbills and storksbills) and the Vetch family (birds foot trefoil, tufted vetch,) will all germinate more easily if they have undergone vernalisation. Some Umbellifers, for example sweet cicely, also benefit from winter sowing. Those species requiring vernalisation will be shown as Seed Type **V**.

Scarification

Other species with hard seed coats may require scarification. Here it is the abrasive action of the soil that breaks down the seed coat over time. Sometimes a combination of scarification and vernalisation will speed up the germination of these species. We can mimic this action by rubbing the seeds briefly between two pieces of fine sandpaper before sowing. Again the Vetch or Pea family benefit from this process. Without it some species may take several years to germinate. Those requiring scarification are Seed Type **S**

Other conditions which may be required: light, fresh seed, or wet conditions

As you might expect, there are more germination requirements that we need to take into account. The most surprising of these is the need for light to trigger germination of certain species. Poppies in particular, and some other wildflowers will only germinate if, in wild conditions, the seed has been exposed to light. This happens during ploughing and can explain why poppies may sometimes appear in prolific numbers, quite unexpectedly, when the soil is disturbed in this way. These species should be sown on the surface of compost or grit if you are using it, or sown directly onto the soil and gently pressed in. (Seed Type **L**). Yet other species will only germinate well if the seed is sown as soon as it is ripe, before dormancy sets in. (Seed Type **F**). Lastly, some of our wetland plants require very wet soil, which is not allowed to dry out at all. (Seed Type **W**). Those requiring no special treatment are Seed Type **N**.

General instructions

Once these conditions are taken into account, germination is easy! Use a soil based compost, of a John Innes type. In general, wildflowers prefer to grow in soil, rather than one of the peat substitutes such as coir. You can use your own garden soil with a very small amount of home made compost added, but you may get germination of weed seedlings which can be confusing. Often a 9 centimetre pot is sufficient to provide you with a huge number of seedlings. Simply fill the pot with compost and firm gently. After scarification (if required) scatter the seed as evenly and finely as possible on the soil surface and then cover with a very thin layer of horticultural grit. This will deter fungal diseases such as 'damping off', which can cause rapid seedling death. If the seed is exceptionally fine (foxgloves, wild marjoram) or requires light to germinate sow the tiny seeds **on top** of the grit. They will fall into spaces without being completely covered up and so a little light can enter.

Once the seed is sown, leave the pots outside in a place where they will benefit either from winter weather conditions if they require vernalisation, or from spring sunshine if they do not. For those species requiring wet conditions, place the pots in containers full of water, to come halfway up the side of the pot and ensure that the container does not dry out.

Germination may take several months, and don't expect all the seeds to germinate at the same time. But once the seedlings appear and are large enough to handle (this will vary considerably with species) prick them out into pots or plugs and grow them on in a sheltered place. You will need to water them in dry conditions. They can then be put into their permanent positions, in meadow areas, borders, rock gardens or pond edges, in late spring.

Collecting your own seed

The Wildlife and Countryside Act of 1981 made it illegal to uproot plants from the wild, but it is not illegal to collect seed except of certain protected species. However, you are still depleting a natural resource and seed collection of any species in the wild is not recommended. Buy your seeds from a reputable seed supplier (see the end of this booklet). That way, you can be sure that you are getting the species you want, and are not contributing to the loss of species in the wild. Once you have established a wildflower in your garden, it will produce all the seed you could need for propagating more plants, with enough to pass on to friends.

It is also important to plant your wildflowers in your own garden only, or on your own land. Introducing wildflowers into areas where they do not naturally occur can influence the survival of the species already established there.

Plant notes

Each plant described has its English and Latin names and details of the flowering time, height of the plant and germination type.

A gravelled area with cottage garden plants and wildflowers

FOUR

Plants for rock or scree gardens

Dry stony habitats in the wild

In the wild, dry habitats occur in a large number of places. Cliff tops, shingle beaches, lowland heaths and chalk or limestone grasslands all have their own special plants that thrive in dry conditions. We also have mountains in North Wales, Cumbria and Scotland, where true 'alpines' grow. Many plants in these habitats are small and neat, making them ideal subjects for gravel areas, raised beds, paving or small containers.

Chalk and limestone grasslands are declining rapidly, as old grassland is ploughed up, or traditional sheep grazing is no longer carried out. These areas are very rich, and a single square metre may contain forty or fifty different plant species. Some of these special plants can be enjoyed in the garden and are very suitable for warm, dry spots – indeed they will often thrive where other garden varieties will not. The pasque flower, small scabious, birds foot trefoil and perennial flax are all wildflowers from poor grassland habitats that adapt very well to garden cultivation. From the seaside habitats, sea campion and yellow stonecrop are ideally suited to gravel or scree gardens, raised beds or containers.

Looking after your rock garden plants

Garden rockeries are rather out of fashion now, probably due to their very artificial look. It is difficult to construct a rock garden that looks anywhere near as good as the real thing, and it is probably easier to make a scree area for some of the plants in this section. This need not be on a slope, but should be well drained and in full sun. Dig in some grit before planting to improve drainage. Plant in spring or autumn, and mulch the whole area around the plants with grit or gravel. This will improve its appearance, making it look more natural and help to suppress weeds. Wildlife too will benefit as gravel warms quickly in the sun, making it an ideal basking spot for butterflies or lizards. Lizards can be further encouraged by incorporating lengths of plastic pipe in the construction, to provide safe hiding places. If a few large rocks are included, toads may use the damp spots beneath them. Some of the smaller species mentioned will also grow happily in containers such as half wooden barrels. Again, a gravel mulch aids drainage and suppresses weeds.

Perennial Flax - *Linum perenne*

Bird's Foot Trefoil - *Lotus corniculatus*

Pasque Flower - *Pulsatilla vulgaris*

Sea Campion - *Silene uniflora*

Small Scabious - *Scabiosa columbaria*

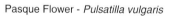

Pasque Flower

Pulsatilla vulgaris

Perennial April-June 15-25cms Seed Type **F**

The Pasque flower is one of our rarest and most colourful wildflowers and has been grown in gardens for generations. It is declining in the wild, as its natural habitats - sunny slopes on short chalk and limestone grasslands - disappear. In cultivation it is not terribly fussy about its growing conditions, and thrives in full sun in a light soil that is either alkaline or neutral. Its name comes from the Old French for Eastertide, as it flowers around this time. The velvety petals are bright purple and surround the golden yellow pollen bearing stamens which attract bees. The leaves are pale green and delicately ferny and the flowers are followed by pretty fluffy seed heads. The long flowering period plus attractive seed heads make this a perfect plant for a gravel garden or raised bed. There are garden varieties with flowers of wine red or white.

Many legends surround this species. The country name 'Dane's Blood' suggested that it grew where there had been great battles. Its green dye has been used in the past to colour the shells of Easter eggs.

Perennial Flax

Linum perenne

Perennial May-June 30-60cms Seed Type **N**

The simple, open sky blue flowers of this plant make it a perfect example of an elegant wildflower that deserves a sunny place in every garden. The petals close at midday, so a well-drained soil with morning sun is necessary to enjoy it at its best. The branched stems are slender and wavy, so plant it close to a path to appreciate the colour and movement of the groups of five petalled flowers. The flowers attract the odd butterfly and are not obscured by the delicate pale green leaves.

In the wild it is another rare plant of well-drained grassland habitats which are declining rapidly. It will grow in thin grass, but in the garden it is much more likely to survive in gravel, or between paving stones. Although a perennial plant, it is relatively short lived and it is wise to collect seed in August for sowing the next spring if the plant mysteriously disappears. In very dry conditions, where the seedlings are not overwhelmed by other more robust plants, it will self seed reliably. The name flax comes from the Old English word *fleax*, meaning to twist or weave into cloth.

Bird's Foot Trefoil
Lotus corniculatus
Perennial May-August 10-30cms Seed Type **SV**

This is one of the most valuable plants we can grow to support butter-flies. The common blue and brown argus feed on the nectar from the dainty yellow and orange flowers. The common blue and the five and six spot burnet moths, lay their eggs on the leaves. Bird's foot trefoil can be grown in short grass, in a sunny well-drained raised bed or rock garden.

Bird's foot trefoil has almost more common names than any other British wildflower. Over 70 have been recorded with Tom Thumb and eggs and bacon being the most common. Tom Thumb was a small magi-cal sprite and this was his flower. Its association with witchcraft or luck is reflected in a Irish name – no blame – as carrying this plant with you to school meant that you would not be punished for your wrong doings!

In the wild, bird s foot trefoil is still widespread and can be found in many situations, including short grassland, roadside verges and heathland. It prefers the sun, and will flower through most of the summer. In the garden it can be relied upon to attract some of our most beautiful small butterflies and a range of native bees.

Small Scabious
Scabiosa columbaria
Perennial July-September 15-35cms Seed Type **N**

This plant's name comes from its former use to treat 'all scabby infec-tions' and John Gerard's Herbal of 1597 reports its effectiveness against 'the biting of serpents and stingings of venomous beasts'! Now though we can include it in our gardens to encourage butterflies, particularly the small tortoiseshell. Solitary mining bees and honeybees are also drawn to the nectar it produces.

Its natural habitat is chalk grassland. In the garden it will reach a greater size than in the wild, and will flower prolifically in a dry, sunny spot, seeding into gravel or between paving stones. From July to Sep-tember the whole plant is topped with masses of beautiful lilac flowers, providing late summer nectar for a range of insects. This is important for those butterflies that overwinter as hibernating adults, so including this plant in the garden can assist in the their survival . The seed heads are as pretty as the flowers and finches find them irresistible. Sow the separated seeds either in the autumn or spring.

Sea Campion
Silene uniflora
Perennial May-August 10-20cms Seed type **N**

There are few wildflowers that are entirely suitable for containers in a small patio garden, but this is one of them. Providing the compost is well drained, this little plant will flower for many months, and because of its slightly sprawling nature, will drape itself elegantly over the side of a pot or hanging basket. In the wild, sea campion's white bells can be seen on cliffs and shingle.

The flowers are quite large for the size of the plant itself. They are pure white and behind each one is an inflated calyx, similar to that of bladder campion. The smooth grey green leaves form a dense mat and the large flowers are held daintily above them in a nodding habit.   Some leaves are retained through the winter, making a damp habitat for soil creatures such as beetles and earthworms. In the spring, this mat of leaves can be removed, to encourage a flush of new young growth.

All campions are attractive to bees, and some moth species will visit the flowers for nectar. The campion moth lays its eggs on the flower buds and the nocturnal caterpillars feed on the seeds as they develop, moving to the leaves when the seeds have all gone.

Yellow Stonecrop
Sedum acre
Perennial May-July 2-10cms Seed Type **N**

Biting stonecrop and wall pepper are names that reflect the fact that this edible plant has a hot peppery taste, and was eaten as a spring salad in years gone by. Other names, including 'come home husband however drunk you be' are rather more fanciful! Its occasional presence on rooftops gave rise to the superstition that it protected dwellings from lightning.

In May and June the many bright yellow star shaped flowers of this tiny plant are still a familiar sight on the tops of walls, or even alongside motorways, where the verge may be dry and almost nothing else will grow. Beekeepers value this plant for the nectar it provides, and in the garden it will thrive in the hottest driest spot in a gravel garden, between stones or paving, or on old walls. Its fleshy leaves store water, enabling it to deal with dry conditions. Try growing this plant in a dry spot with wild thyme – the contrasting flower colours of yellow and purple, are quite spectacular.

Yellow Stonecrop - *Sedum acre*

FIVE

Plants for light shade

Shady habitats in the wild

There can hardly be a garden in the country that does not have a difficult shady spot where very little will grow. We may despair of finding anything to thrive in a situation like this, but there are lots of wildflowers that are tolerant of light shade, even where the soil may be dry and exhausted of nutrients. In general they are the plants of wild hedgerows and copses and most of these plants flower in spring. They bring a breath of fresh air to the wildflower garden when we need it most.

Country hedgerows

The importance of hedgerows as habitats in our countryside cannot be over-stressed and in spite of new plantings, old hedges are still being removed, making a steady loss. Hedgerows are fantastic places for wildlife, providing shelter for small mammals, food and nesting places for birds such as the song thrush or blackbird and a habitat for lots of insects including one of our most rare and beautiful native butterflies – the black hairstreak. In the garden a hedge can be equally inviting to your wildlife visitors, provided you include a wide range of native shrubs such as hawthorn, blackthorn, dogwood and guelder rose, together with native climbers like wild honeysuckle, dog rose and bramble. Include some wildflowers in the light shade beneath and your hedgerow habitat is complete.

An old established hedge of privet or *Lonicera* – both commonly used for hedging – can be greatly improved by the inclusion of some wildflowers at its base. Red campion, sweet violet and primrose will all grow in this situation. Planting wildflowers under Leyland cypress is another matter, because this tree dries the soil even more than the nutrient hungry privet. As a wildlife habitat Leyland cypress hedges can actually be quite good, providing dense foliage for nesting birds, and encouraging goldcrests to the garden, but it is absolutely essential to keep this hedge regularly cut to 2 – 3 metres, which is hard work. Never plant this species unless you are prepared for the maintenance it requires, several times a year. Beneath it, only a few wildflowers will grow, but it is worth trying wild strawberry and sweet woodruff, which can cope with the lack of moisture.

Native woodlands

Our woodlands are famed the world over for their beauty. Coppice woodland, where bluebells and stitchwort abound is rich in wildlife, particularly butterflies. Here the standard trees may be oak or ash, and the shrubs beneath, usually hazel, are cut on a rotational basis, every 12 or 15 years. This allows light to penetrate to the ground, rejuvenating the woodland flora. In our gardens, we may prune hedges and shrubs quite drastically without endangering the survival of any woodland wildflowers we may have planted.

Shrub borders can also mimic the hedgerow or woodland habitat, providing the shade that these wildflowers love. A border of Buddleia with stitchwort and campion beneath will not only look attractive, but will encourage butterflies and moths to the garden.

All the woodland and hedgerow wildflowers are easy to grow and manage. Leaves will naturally fall from the trees and shrubs above them, providing a nutrient rich mulch. The biennial foxgloves will need to seed, so try to ensure that there is not too much disturbance around them. In general, all these plants are best left to themselves.

A cool shady place for bluebells and other wildflowers

Bluebell - *Scilla non-scripta*

Red Campion - *Silene dioica*

Sweet Violet - *Viola odorata*

Stinking Hellebore -
Helleborus foetidus

Foxglove - *Digitalis purpurea*

Bluebell
Scilla non-scripta
Perennial April-June 25-30cms Seed type **V**

This is one of our most familiar and recognisable wildflowers. In May it can cover the ground beneath beech trees, or under oaks and hazel in coppice woodland, with sheets of hazy blue not seen anywhere else in the world. In the garden, grow it in light shade, in short grass beneath a tree or under a hedge. The name bluebell has only been in general use since the early 19th Century. English hyacinth was the more usual name, although many country names, particularly cuckoo flower, or cuckoo's boots were commonly used for these sweetly scented flowers.

In the spring their strap like green leaves emerge from a perennial bulb and are followed by a robust stem with up to twenty flowers, all nodding in the same direction. Honey bees find the nectar not by the usual route which rather too small for them, but by pushing their way into the back of the flower. Some butterflies will also take the nectar.

Wholesale stripping of bluebells from the wild is still a huge problem. Ensure that your bulbs come from a legitimate supplier. Seed will germinate easily after a cold winter, but the little plants take several years to flower.

Red Campion
Silene dioica
Perennial April-July 30-100cms Seed type **N**

A versatile plant for light shade, red campion is also happy in more sunny places. At the hedge bottom, with bluebells and stitchwort, the combination of pink, white and blue can be quite stunning. The flowers are borne in profusion above a mat of robust hairy leaves and the dark seeds form in a cup shaped seedpod. Seed sown in spring, will result in plants flowering that same summer. Once the first flush of flowers has finished, the whole plant can be cut back to produce another flowering which may continue right into the autumn. Two moths, the lychnis and the twin spot carpet commonly lay their eggs on red campion. The caterpillars of the latter feed on the foliage and flowers while the lychnis caterpillar eats the campion seeds and often lives inside the seed pod!

This is a familiar wildflower associated with bad luck, witches and snakes sometimes called snake plant, mother die and adder's flower.

Sweet Violet
Viola odorata
Perennial February-April 5-10cms Seed type **V**

This wildflower is aptly named, as its strong but fleeting scent is incredibly sweet. The dark purple flowers are quite large and are held above the hairy, heart shaped leaves. Sweet violet flowers very early, sometimes before its pollinating insects are out and about. Both bees and butterflies will visit it, but the second small flush of flowers in July is more likely to produce seed from self-pollination. Look out then for the swelling seedpods, with the rather large white seeds developing inside and collect them when the pods split open. They are best sown in the early winter, to germinate in profusion the following spring. If left to their own devices, the plants will also spread naturally by runners.

In the past this plant was a common remedy for headaches and insomnia – indeed the sugared violets that are still sold as sweets or to decorate cakes were a remnant of this former use. The leaves have also been made into a poultice to treat cancerous growths.

Stinking Hellebore
Helleborus foetidus
Perennial January-May 50-60cms Seed type **V**

Stinking hellebore is a beautiful wildflower, also known as bear's foot on account of the shape of its deeply divided, glossy, dark green leaves. In the wild it can be found beneath beech and yew trees, flourishing in deep shade on dry soils. This indicates how useful it can be in the garden, not just in lightly shady places, but in much heavier shade too. The bell-shaped nodding flowers are lime green tipped with maroon, and brighten the darkest corner. Each flowering stem may have ten or more large flowers held above the dark evergreen foliage. Both bumblebees and honeybees collect the early pollen, making it a valuable wildlife plant. It can flower for many months, and the blooms are replaced by light green swollen seedpods, full of shiny black seeds. Sow these in the autumn, as they will only germinate after a good period of cold weather.

The plant leaves do have a foetid smell as the Latin name suggests, but only when they are touched or bruised. In the past this hellebore was commonly grown as a treatment for worms in children - how-

ever its action was dangerously violent and fatalities sometimes oc-
curred. Plant out of harms way in a shady corner.

Foxglove
Digitalis purpurea
Biennial May-July 100-150cms Seed type **L**

Tall, stately and colourful, the foxglove is a familiar and much loved wildflower, ideal for garden cultivation. It thrives in slightly acid soils, but in
alkaline conditions an organic mulch will provide the humus it requires.
There are many garden varieties in rich colours but our native pink
flower, each with its spotted throat, can hardly be beaten. It is a biennial – producing a rosette of grey green woolly leaves in its first year and
flowers in the second. If the flowering spike is removed as the seeds are
setting it may well continue for a third year. The large pink bells are ar-
ranged down one side of the tall stem and in June they hum with bumblebees. Several moth species lay their eggs on the leaves.

Foxgloves will naturalise in light shade under trees, either in borders or in short grass. They look wonderful along the shady side of a
hedge, but can be quite happy in sun as well.   Allow them to self-seed
where you want them, or increase them by sowing the minute seeds in
pots in the autumn, with the seed hardly covered. Put the small plants
out in the spring where you want them to flower.

In English folklore this plant has many associations with fairies
and witchcraft, hence the local names fairies' thimbles or fairies' gloves.
Children were told that foxes used the flowers on their paws to enable
them to reach the hen house invisibly or in silence.   The heart drug, di-
goxin was once extracted from the leaves of our own foxglove. Now the
Mediterranean species woolly foxglove, *Digitalis lanata,* is the usual
source of this powerful heart drug.

Primrose
Primula vulgaris
Perennial March-May 8-15cms Seed type **V**

The primrose acquired its common name from 'prime rose' meaning the
first flower of spring, and was traditionally gathered as a posy on Mother-
ing Sunday. A great deal of superstition surrounds the plant, particularly
with regard to health. It was thought not to thrive around villages where

the Great Plague had taken lives and its appearance in early spring brought a happy optimism for the warm days ahead.

Once the primrose was one of our most common wildflowers. The practice of uprooting it for gardens depleted our native stock considerably, but now numbers are starting to build up again in some habitats. It was commonly found around every village in hedgebanks and woodland, particularly on heavy clay soils, and in the garden it prefers a heavy or rich soil.

The pale yellow, notched petals have a delicate scent that attracts early butterflies and moths, the latter pollinating the flowers at night. Each flower is borne on a single stem which arises from the crinkled green leaves – the odd primrose flower may be seen in January - and it will continue to produce flowers sporadically into the late spring.

The ideal place for primroses in the garden is a hedge bottom, or on a slightly shady bank, although if they are grown in grass care must be taken not to mow until the seed has been shed sometime in May or June. The seedlings will appear the following spring and may not flower for another year. Seed may be sown in pots in the autumn or winter and left outside for best germination results.

Primrose - *Primula vulgaris*

SIX

Plants for meadows

Wild meadow habitats

Most of us have read at some time that in the last 50 years we have lost over 95 percent of our hay meadows. They have been sprayed with herbicides, or ploughed up to make way for vast green swathes of rye grass, winter wheat or oil seed rape. These colourful tapestries of grasses and wildflowers, with all their attendant butterflies, beetles, bumblebees and other creatures are now rarely seen. Where they remain, they are cherished as unique habitats.

The term 'meadow' brings to mind different images: green, wet grass full of spring cowslips and ladies smock, or tall dry grasses intermingled with scabious and knapweed. Every meadow may be different in its underlying soil type, species composition, time of flowering, and the wildlife that lives there. This means that for our gardens, whatever the natural conditions, there are suitable meadow wildflowers that will thrive in grass. And that is the key to this type of gardening. A meadow is mainly a mixture of grass species, with a few colourful wildflowers thrown in. The grasses are crucial to the habitat as a whole.

Not all wildflowers can survive in this grassy habitat. Those that can are generally perennial plants that have evolved to flower and seed in the spring or early summer although there are a few really useful late flowerers. More important is the fact that they can survive being cut down, and possibly trampled by cows or sheep. Popular annual wildflowers such as poppies and cornflowers are plants of disturbed habitats with patches of bare soil such as field margins. These pretty species struggle to hold their own in meadow grass, and generally fail, but they do have a place in garden borders or can be sown as a 'cornfield mixture' in a sunny spot.

There are lots of very attractive wildflowers that will grow in grass. Some early flowering species are mentioned in the 'Plants for Damp Spots' chapter and some others are described here.

Garden meadows

It is only possible to make a 'meadow effect' in a garden. In the wild meadow the community of species that produces the haze of grass seedheads and flowers will have taken many years to develop and we can only create an approximation of that in cultivation. However, it can still be a stunning garden feature, but there must be a large commitment to create and maintain it successfully. Meadows are best grown from good mixed seed from a reputable supplier, sown on weed-free low fertility soil. They must be cut (not mown) in late summer and the hay raked off. Meadows are a lot of work!

If however you have an area of fine lawn grass in the garden, it is possible to recreate a meadow effect by planting a range of small seed grown wildflowers as plug plants, and following a meadow maintenance regime of cutting and raking. The six plants profiled below will all survive lawn grass that is not rich in rye grass or other tough species. Greater knapweed, field scabious, cowslip and meadow cranesbill will even hold their own in tougher grass such as couch.

Meadow wildlife

A meadow in the garden will have a range of exciting wildlife. The flower species encourage the insects already mentioned, but long grass has other things to offer. Several species of butterfly, in particular meadow brown, ringlet, small and large skipper, gatekeeper and marbled white, lay their eggs on a selection of meadow grasses. Many other insects such as moths, beetles, grasshoppers and crickets will make their homes here. Field voles and mice, shrews and hedgehogs all search for food and find shelter in meadows. Many birds forage for the insects and the grass and flower seeds that are plentiful in this habitat. In short, an area - however small - of long grass and wildflowers in your garden, will make a huge difference to the numbers and types of wildlife visitors.

Moon Daisy - *Leucanthemum vulgare*

Cowslip - *Primula veris*

Hoary Plantain - *Plantago media*

Field Scabious
- *Knautia arvensis*

Meadow Cranesbill - *Geranium pratense*   Greater Knapweed - *Centaurea scabiosa*

Moon Daisy
Leucanthemum vulgare
Perennial May-July 30-80cms Seed type **N**

Moon daisy, marguerite, ox eye daisy and dog daisy are all familiar common names for this wildflower. The white petals earn it an association with the moon as the flowers appear to glow in the evening light, but the name dog daisy comes from the rather unpleasant smell! A bunch of these flowers in the porch was thought to ward off lightning.

In the wild it is still a common plant of roadsides, hedge bottoms and old hay meadows. It is a short lived perennial and thus only really thrives where there is a certain amount of disturbance and some bare soil to allow self seeding. It can be very prolific, and its white flowers with their central yellow disks can completely dominate a habitat for a year or two before it settles down to coexist happily with other flowers and grasses. Grow it in full sun, or in light shade alongside a hedge.

This lovely plant is a joy in its own right, but it is also a good insect attractant for a wildlife garden. Several of the meadow butterflies will take nectar from it, including small tortoiseshell and marbled white and it is a major resource for several species of solitary bee which specialise on pollens from the daisy family.

Cowslip
Primula veris
Perennial April-May 15-30cms Seed type **V**

The cowslip is about the most versatile wildflower we can plant in our gardens. It will thrive in sun or light shade, dry or damp soils and, most importantly, will grow happily in grass as well as in borders. Its nodding yellow freckled flowers are delicious scented and they stand well above the crinkled leaves, providing colour in the garden through April and May. Once the seedpods have dried, seed may be collected and sown fresh, but it is easier to germinate if it is sown in the autumn and left out in the cold through the winter. Alternatively divide the roots of existing plants after flowering. In the wild the cowslip is spreading from its damp meadow habitats and establishing on roadside verges where bees may collect the pollen and it is safe from picking or spraying.

Cowslips held an important place in our country lore. Flowers were gathered in spring to make cowslip balls, or 'tisty-tosties' used as children's playthings, or decorations. The name actually derives from 'cowslop' as it was assumed that the flowers sprang up wherever a cow pat was deposited! A more endearing name is St Peter's Keys, as the blooms were thought to represent the keys to the gates of Heaven.

Field Scabious
Knautia arvensis
Perennial July-September 30-60cms Seed type **N**

The large flowers of field scabious are made up of many tiny pale mauve florets that blend wonderfully with other late blooming meadow plants and grasses. It can cope quite well in tough grass, and in the wild is a fairly common plant of roadsides especially on free draining soils. In the garden it is adaptable, and looks equally at home in a sunny border as in a meadow, contrasting well with greater knapweed, which also flowers at this time. It has other country names, particularly gypsy rose.

In the wildlife garden it is a very valuable plant, providing nectar for a wide range of bees and a variety of butterfly species into the late summer. Indeed there will often be a few flowers as late as October, and after that the seed heads are an attractive feature. Seed may be collected whenever the flowers have gone over and the seed heads look dry. The seed germinates easily but erratically in spring, especially in well drained compost, and it will do so on its own in a gravel path if it gets the chance.

Hoary Plantain
Plantago media
Perennial May-August 15-30cms Seed type **N**

It may seem rather strange to find a species of plantain recommended for growing in the garden, but this is not the ordinary 'rat's tails' so often found in lawns (*Plantago laceolata* or *Plantago major*). The hoary plantain is a beautiful plant, with neat rosettes of grey-green leaves, and a scented flower spike. The single flowerhead is creamy white with pale lilac or pink anthers, giving the whole plant a delicate fluffy appearance. It looks equally as good at the front of a border as in short meadow grass. In the wild it can be found in dry grassy places, especially on free-draining soils. This species prefers a sunny spot, and once established the leaf rosettes slowly clump up and spread to form small colonies. These can be very easily separated and the resultant plantlets moved in the autumn. Alternatively, seed can be sown in spring and germinates quite readily.

Hoary plantain can attract a range of wildlife visitors to the garden. Some finches enjoy the seeds, and bees will collect the pollen. Several moth species use plantain leaves as their larval food plant. It is also known as cotton flower, and in the past gardeners used the leaves to stop bleeding from small cuts.

Meadow Cranesbill
Geranium pratense
Perennial June August 30-80cms Seed type **SV**

The largest of our native geraniums is an easy garden subject. It will grow in sun or light shade in a border, and in quite tough meadow grass. It has been cultivated as a garden plant for many years, on account of its beautiful bowl shaped violet-blue flowers and its undemanding nature. Several of the hardy garden geraniums, including white and double forms and the well known varieties Mrs Kendall Clark and Silver Queen, are derived from our wild meadow cranesbill.

In the meadow it adds an early splash of blue, just when many white and pink flowers are coming into their own. The deeply divided leaves are attractive at all times and take on a red hue in the autumn. The seedpods – the cranesbills of the common name – are sharply pointed, and as the seed ripens they split open, curl back, and catapult the seed for some distance to spread the plant effectively. Finches, particularly bullfinches, enjoy the seeds of wild geraniums. Solitary bees, bumblebees and butterflies, especially the skippers, also visit this plant, making it indispensable in the wildlife garden.

Where there are dry limestone soils in the wild, this plant can occur in profusion. In some southern counties large areas of the locally named blue buttons can be seen on roadside verges. In the garden any dry spot will keep it more than happy.

Greater Knapweed
Centaurea scabiosa
Perennial July-September 30-90cms Seed type **N**

No meadow is complete without the greater knapweed, bringing colour and wildlife to the garden right through until September. Butterflies and bees love this plant and it is also a goldfinch magnet, along with its cousin the lesser knapweed. In a meadow or rough grass it is undemanding. The purple flowers are borne on stiff stems above the deeply lobed leaves. The flowers themselves are made up of many tiny florets and the outer ring of these has longer, more divided petals giving the flower a pretty frilly appearance. Once the flowers have set seed, the beautiful shiny seedpod opens at the top to tempt goldfinches with the large pale seeds inside. Bees collect pollen and nectar from the flowers, and many species of butterfly visit throughout the flowering period.

In the garden greater knapweed prefers a soil that drains well, either in full sun or some light shade. It is an easy plant to grow from seed, requiring no special treatment and seeds sown in early spring will flower the same year. In the wild it grows in rough grassy places, such as roadsides and alongside hedgerows, as long as the soil is dry.

A wildflower meadow with wild grasses and many species of wildflower

SEVEN

Plants for damp spots

Wild, wet habitats

Really wild, wet habitats in our countryside are now few and far between. Flood meadows have been drained to extend the range of agricultural crops they will produce. Farm ponds are no longer necessary, and have been filled in or have dried up. Rivers and ditches are dredged to keep the water flowing at all times to prevent flooding. Hand in hand with the steady loss of these wet places, has been the decline of our beautiful wetland flora.

Wet gardens

In the garden one solution to a wet lawn is to install expensive drainage, but wet conditions can provide an opportunity not to be missed. This is a situation where working with your natural conditions, rather than against them, is the answer to the 'problem'. A damp lawn full of ladies smock, ragged robin, snakeshead fritillary and bugle is a stunning sight, and creating an area such as this not only cuts down on gardening costs, but on labour too.

A wet 'meadow' will need some care and maintenance. To get started, small plants, especially those grown from seed, can be introduced into fine lawn grass in much the same way as bulbs, and a bulb planter is a useful tool for this. In the autumn, simply take out a little plug of soil and settle the plant into the space. Fritillary bulbs will need to be planted at a depth of 5 cms or so. All the plants mentioned are early flowerers, so grass and plants can be cut when the seeds have been shed – generally by late June and the resultant crop of hay raked off. You can then continue to cut the area through the summer but make sure it is not cropped too short. In the spring simply allow everything to grow up and flower again.

A garden bog

In drier ground it is still possible to grow some of these attractive species. A pond, although a fantastic wildlife resource, may not be for you particularly if you have children using the garden. A bog garden may be a better option and can be very simply made with an off-cut of flexible pond lining material such as butyl rubber. In a sunny or slightly shaded spot, dig a saucer shaped hole to a depth of about 40cms and line it with the material. Spike a few holes into the bottom with the garden fork as some drainage will be necessary. Fill the area with your garden soil enriched with good organic compost and water well before planting your chosen species. If you can arrange for the rainwater runoff from the house roof or a garden building to drain into your bog, so much the better.

One of the advantages of growing some of our native wetland species is that they are incredibly adaptable. Most of those mentioned will grow in good moisture retentive soil or in several inches of standing water. If you already have a pond, there are lots of wildflowers suitable for the pond edge habitat. Many of these are colourful gems that are also good insect attractants, so planting them will also enhance the wildlife-friendly nature of your garden.

A damp pond edge is ideal for purple loosestrife, water mint and other wildflowers preferring damp soil.

Lady's Smock - *Cardamine pratensis*

Water Mint - *Mentha aquatica*

Snake's Head Fritillary - *Fritillaria meleagris*

Ragged Robin - *Lychnis flos-cuculi*

Purple Loosestrife
- *Lythrum salicaria*

Lady's Smock
Cardamine pratensis
Perennial April-June 15-30cms Seed type **W**

It is always worthwhile to plant the larval food plants of butterflies, even if the plants themselves are not the most attractive. Lady's smock however is not only one of our prettiest spring flowers, but the food plant of two butterflies which will breed in the garden – the green veined white and the orange tip. The orange tip lays its eggs on the flower heads in May or June. They quickly hatch and the caterpillars closely resemble the green seedpods on which they feed.

The flowers of lady's smock are a delicate shade of lilac, with slightly deeper lilac veins. In the wild they can cover large areas in damp meadows, and will spread well in the garden in the right conditions. This plant does not need full sun, but will appreciate soil that does not dry out, so the pond edge, a bog garden or very damp fine grass will suit it well. The leaves are edible and have a peppery taste. Sow seed of this plant in spring or autumn and ensure that it stays damp. Alternatively, it can be increased by laying its leaves on damp compost, where they will root and produce new small plantlets.

Lady's smock has many other country names and is well known as milkmaids, or cuckoo flower. Several other plants share this name, as their blossoming was thought to herald the arrival of the cuckoo in April.

Water Mint
Mentha aquatica
Perennial July-September 15-60cms **WL**

Water mint is a very adaptable plant, flourishing in the damp soil of a bog garden, or in water up to depth of 10 or 12 cms. Its tight clusters of tiny rosy pink flowers are seen in the late summer and like so many members of the Labiate family, it is a very valuable source of nectar for butterflies and bees. Like all mints, its greeny-purple leaves and stems spread very quickly in full sun or light shade. On the pond edge the stems can easily be removed in the autumn, but in a bog garden the water mint may spread too rapidly for some tastes!

Often called horse mint, this plant is still common and widespread, and can be found growing alongside streams or in boggy ground where it produces a sweet minty smell when trodden upon. In the garden, plant it somewhere accessible, so that the leaves can be crushed on passing.

The seed is not easy to germinate and requires wet soil and only the lightest covering of grit, but this is such an easy plant to propagate from any piece of stem, that it is hardly worth bothering with the tiny seeds.

Snake's Head Fritillary
Fritillaria meleagris
Perennial April-May 20-40cms Seed Type **V**

To see the snake's head fritillary in the wild is a privilege. It is a rare plant of Central and Southern England, surviving only in protected places and nature reserves. Where it does occur it grows in profusion, and a meadow full of its nodding bells is a magical sight. There is some doubt as to whether it is a true native, as references to it in the ancient herbals are few, but its once widespread distribution in water meadows indicates that it must have been a locally common plant. Many counties have their own special name for the fritillary, suggesting that it grew in many more locations than it does now. The names reflect the chequered nature of the flowers, likened to snake's scales, (snake's head, snake's head lily), or the feathers of guinea fowl (guinea hen flower). Wherever it grew its beauty was celebrated, often with special 'snake's head Sundays' when children would pick and distribute the flowers in small posies to local inhabitants.

We can grow this plant easily in the garden in a good rich soil and it will spread quickly in fine grass. Although it produces seed in profusion, seedlings may take five or six years to reach flowering size, so it is best to plant bulbs purchased from a reputable source. Plant them in the autumn, and they will reward you with a stunning display the following spring. The chequered purple or pure white flowers are pollinated by bumblebees and are held singly above the thin strap shaped leaves. If the bulbs are grown in grass, ensure that it is not cut until the seeds have fallen in June.

Ragged Robin
Lychnis flos-cuculi
Perennial May-August 30-50cms Seed Type **N**

The name of this plant is confusing, as the Latin, *flos-cuculi*, means cuckoo flower, although that name is more generally used for the lady s smock. However, several plants bore the name cuckoo flower if they came into bloom in April or May. Ragged robin was also known as wild william, to distinguish it from the garden sweet william, which, like ragged robin, is a member of the pink family.

This is an easy wildflower to grow as long as it has soil that is not too dry. It self seeds well, will grow in damp grass and flowers over a long period – altogether an ideal garden subject. The branched flowering head consists of a cluster of flowers and the deeply divided pink petals have almost a shredded look, giving the whole plant a delicate and wild appearance.

Ragged robin is pollinated by butterflies and some species of long tongued bee, so is a good wildlife attractant. The campion moth and lychnis moth also use this as their larvae food plant. Other moths take nectar from its flowers at night. In the garden it looks at its best in a damp meadow, but is at home in a bog garden or on a pond edge, even in light shade. Drainage of its preferred damp habitats has led to serious decline of this plant in the countryside.

Purple Loosestrife
Lythrum salicaria
Perennial June-September 30-50cms Seed Type **LW**

This wetland plant shared its descriptive common country name of long purples with the early purple orchid, but the name loosestrife is altogether more fascinating. A nosegay of the flowers was thought to prevent or stop quarrelling and thus to lose strife. It was a plant of river and stream banks or marshy areas where its tall spikes of purple flowers were a common sight. In the garden we can grow it in any good soil that is moisture retentive – it does not have to be in wet ground. The seeds are minute and best sown without covering and kept well watered. However the purple loosestrife self seeds well, on the pond edge, bog garden or even in a mixed garden border if the soil is reasonably rich.

Purple loosestrife is an excellent wildlife plant, attracting bees to its pollen and nectar. Butterflies, too, enjoy the nectar if the conditions are still and the beautiful small elephant hawkmoth will feed on the leaves. The long clusters of flowers, which arise from stiff, square-plant stalked stems, appear in mid summer and there is often colour from this well into September or even October, the flowers providing valuable late nectar for insects.

Marsh Marigold
Caltha palustris
Perennial March-July 30-40cms Seed Type **WF**

The marsh marigold will only grow in very damp soil and is thus a favourite for the pond edge. Its golden yellow flowers are a joyful sign of spring and the plant has always been held in high regard in country areas where it grows in wet meadows, boggy ground and damp woodland. These places are declining and the marsh marigold with them.

As a garden plant there is little to surpass it for springtime colour in wet soil. The dark green glossy leaves are an attractive feature on their own, but the golden flowers will brighten the garden on the dullest day. Bees forage for both pollen and nectar, making this a good wildlife plant. Fresh seed will germinate well if sown in the late summer and kept very wet.

Kingcup, mollyblobs, water babies and water goggles are some of the many country names for this plant. Also known as mayflower, the blossoms were picked and strewn on doorsteps on April 30th to ward off witches and evil fairies and to bring wealth all year.

Marsh Marigold - *Caltha palustris*

EIGHT

Plants for sunny borders

Most of the wildflowers we have looked at so far have been suitable for quite special places in the garden – meadows, areas beneath shady hedges, bog gardens or rocky places. One thing we should not overlook is that there are many wildflowers that are completely at home amongst other more traditional garden plants and they will add a great deal to the beauty of a mixed herbaceous border, not to mention its wildlife attracting potential. Some of these plants such as Jacob's ladder or musk mallow have been growing in our gardens for many years. Others have been neglected and deserve to be more widely grown.

Wildflowers in cultivation

In the past some of our most attractive native flowers were brought into cultivation and are still with us, albeit in a modified form. White varieties of plants that were naturally blue or pink, such as foxgloves or bluebells were always highly prized and transferred from the wild to gardens. Plants such as violets, with a tendency to produce unusual colour forms or to hybridise amongst themselves were also commonly grown. Naturally occurring double flowered varieties of species such as primrose or red campion were collected from the wild and are still available from specialist plant nurseries. These plants were sometimes less vigorous than their wilder cousins making them suitable for the border, but it is important to remember that double flowered varieties have no nectar or pollen to entice bees or butterflies, so from our point of view are of less interest.

Suitability for borders

The species that work particularly well in borders can come from a variety of natural habitats. One thing they tend to have in common is their slightly restrained nature. Ox eye daisies might look wonderful in a border situation but they have a distinct tendency to take over completely! Growing them in grass will help to curb their natural exuberance. So for borders which may be richer in nutrients than grassy places, and where more space may be available for seeding and spreading, we need to choose our species with care if we want to maintain a border where every plant has a place, and no one species takes over. However, if you prefer your borders to reflect nature and to be wild and luxurious, plant any wildflowers you particularly like!

Nectar borders and their maintenance

Mixed borders with a wide range of insect friendly plants are known as nectar borders, and can be exciting features in any garden. Colourful and buzzing with life, an area with well chosen nectar and pollen plants will add immensely to the wildlife attracting potential of your garden. If wildflowers are also included, this potential is greatly enhanced. Maintenance of a border like this is straightforward. The year's growth should not be cut down in the autumn, but left until March, to allow insects (and sometimes small mammals) to overwinter in safety, to leave seeds for finches, and to enable annual wildflowers such as cornflowers to self seed. In spring the ground can be mulched with organic compost, but this should be used sparingly around the wildflowers. Too rich a soil may encourage some species to produce lots of leaves and not many flowers. Very little else needs to be done, except a little gentle 'weeding' as the summer progresses.

Cornfield gardens

Some of our most colourful wildflowers are annuals once found in profusion in cornfields. These can be sown together in a sunny border to produce a stunning display for several months. A cornfield mix will generally contain cornflowers, corn poppies, corn marigolds and corncockle, together with the little white corn camomile. Sow the seed in spring or autumn, pressing it into the soil rather than covering it. Allow it to grow up and flower and, in September, pull out all the dead flower stalks. Seed will naturally fall to the ground to germinate and continue the display the following year. An area like this will attract many bee species, butterflies, hoverflies and small mammals.

The traditional cornfield flowers - poppies, corn marigold, cornflower and corncockle, are ideal for a sunny border.

Wild Marjoram - *Origanum vulgare*

Cornflower - *Centaurea cyanus*
with Corn Marigold and Corn Camomile

Viper's Bugloss - *Echium vulgare*

Great Mullein - *Verbascum thapsus*

Musk Mallow - *Malva moschata*

Teasel - *Dipsacus fullonum*

Wild Marjoram
Origanum vulgare
Perennial July-September 30-60cms Seed Type **L**

Few wildflowers surpass the wild marjoram for its ability to attract the smaller butterflies to our gardens. Common blue and gatekeeper love this pretty scented plant and bees and bumblebees will also be drawn to it's nectar and pollen. It is an ideal plant for the front of a sunny border, but will also grow in fine grass on well drained soils. It spreads quickly by seed and each individual plant will also clump up until the rootstock may be 60cms across. The small hairy leaves are deliciously scented, with a slightly sweet minty fragrance. The Mediterranean species of *Origanum* are the more usual culinary flavourings, but our wild marjoram is equally as good if picked fresh from the garden. The minute seeds can be sown in the spring and should be left uncovered. At the front of a mixed border, or one reserved exclusively for wildflowers, the clusters of pale pink flowers provide colour and nectar for visiting insects, right through the summer until September.

In the past this plant was gathered from the chalk hillsides and well drained grasslands where it can still be found, to be used as a medicinal cure all. Coughs, kidney complaints, earaches and indigestion were all treated with a tea made from the plant known as joy of the mountain or wild organy. The leaves contain a mild painkiller and a sedative.

Viper's Bugloss
Echium vulgare
Biennial June-September 60-100cms Seed Type **N**

Every part of this plant reminded the ancient herbalists of snakes. The stem is spotted like a snake's skin and the seeds were thought to be shaped like a snake's head. The bright blue flowers unfurl like a coiled viper and the stamens protrude from the trumpet shaped flower just like a snake's tongue. It is not surprising that it was used to treat snake bites!

In the wild it occurs naturally on dry well drained sites, field margins in sandy soil, shingle areas on the coast and gravel pits. In the garden, it will grow on virtually any soil as long as it has its head in the sun.

It is a biennial plant and in the first year produces a rosette of dark green roughly hairy leaves. The tall flower spikes arise in June of the second year, each flowering stalk unfurling its pinky-red buds in succession. The seeds can be collected and sown in spring. Once established, vipers bugloss will drop its large dark grey seeds to produce new plants each year. In the wildlife garden this is a valuable plant, providing nectar for bees, moths and some of the smaller butterflies such as the small and large skippers. Bees are also attracted to its blue pollen. In a sunny border it will provide a striking focal point of towering bright blue spikes, buzzing all summer with insects.

Great Mullein
Verbascum thapsus
Biennial June-August 100-200cms Seed Type **N**

For a tall architectural plant for the back of a sunny border, great mullein or Aaron's rod is hard to beat. For wildlife, it has its own special attraction, as the large open yellow flowers provide nectar and pollen for foraging bees. It is the larval food plant of the mullein moth whose impressive caterpillar is yellow and white with striking black markings.

This biennial is a familiar plant of waste places and roadsides, usually on dry poor soil. In the garden it prefers a sunny well drained spot. Many of its country names refer to the large woolly grey green leaves that appear in the first year, such as poor man's blanket and beggar's blanket. The leaves must indeed be warm – I have found a hibernating hedgehog completely wrapped up in a cosy nest made from the leaves of great mullein! The branched spikes of bright yellow flowers with their orange anthers appear in the second year. It was widely gathered for its medicinal properties and a herbal tobacco made of the leaves was used to cure coughs, bronchitis and asthma.

Mullein produces great quantities of minute seeds and some usually self sow once the plant is established. The seeds, if sown in a pot, need virtually no covering.

Cornflower
Centaurea cyanus
Annual June-September 20-100cms **L**

Not many wildflowers have a colour named after them, but we can all conjure up cornflower blue in our imaginations. The intense bright blue flowers, sometimes called bluebottles, are rarely seen in our fields now having all but disappeared since the 1970s. They were considered to be a serious agricultural weed of wheat or barley and were slowly eradicated. The country name of hurt sickle indicated that it was more than just an annoying weed – it was thought to take the sharp edge off a scythe.

The cornflower is an annual wildflower and is an ideal subject to fill spaces in a mixed border. The seeds can be sown onto the soil surface where they are to flower and gently pressed in – there is no need to cover them. Once established in a border cornflower will self seed freely and always manage to pop up in the most appropriate places. It is a brilliant wildlife plant, attracting many kinds of bees to its nectar and pollen. The common blue butterfly is also greatly attracted to the flowers and goldfinches flock to the silvery seedheads. You can sow the seeds in pots, but as with other annuals, it is easier to sow directly into the soil. For a fantastic display of colour, sow the cornflower with poppies, corn marigold, corncockle and corn camomile to produce a dazzling area of jewel bright colours.

Musk Mallow
Malva moschata
Perennial July-September 30-80cms Seed Type **N**

It is hard to believe that this is one of our native flowers - with such large open pink flowers, it could easily be an exotic garden plant. The saucer shaped blooms are up to 5cms across and have a musky scent. In the wild the single stem may have several flowers up its length, but in the border this plant comes into its own. With a little space and fertile soil it becomes a handsome bushy plant covered with rose pink blossoms right through the late summer. The flowers have both nectar and pollen to attract bees, but this is generally a plant that butterflies ignore. The only exception is the migrant painted lady butterfly which will sometimes lay its eggs on the plant's leaves.

In the wild the musk mallow frequents roadsides and grassy places and does well in the garden in dry soil. It can also be established in a meadow and looks wonderful in grass with the mauve field scabious. In a border its pale pink blooms complement the blue of the cornflower, and grown together they attract a host of different insect species.

Teasel

Dipsacus fullonum

Biennial July-September 30-80cms Seed Type **N**

Architectural plants are much in demand for garden borders and here is a wildflower that performs many functions. It not only adds height and structure to a border, but attracts wildlife into the bargain. Bumblebees, hoverflies and butterflies, particularly peacocks, take the nectar from this plant.

Teasels were once used for 'teasing' or raising the nap of woollen cloth. Our native teasel flower heads have straight spines, so a subspecies with hooked spines, known as fuller's teasel, was more usually grown. Many country names for this plant refer to its brush like nature, including poor man's brush or sweep's brush.

Teasels produce a rosette of bright green spiny leaves in the first year and a tall strong flowering stem in the second. Gerard in his Herbal of 1597 described the plant as having 'heads with sharpe prickles like those of a Hedge-hog'. The tiny flowers appear in a ring around the flower head, and are a pinky-purple colour. The seeds are a favourite with goldfinches, and the plants themselves will stand through to the following year, adding winter interest to the border. Self seeding generally occurs, but seed can be sown in pots, and transplanted before the seedlings have developed tap roots.

In conclusion

This book by no means exhausts the British native wildflowers that are suitable for garden cultivation. Whatever type of garden you have and wherever in the country you live, there are wildflowers suitable for some spot or other in your garden. It is well worth trying other species if you can obtain the seed (or plants) from a grower or plant nursery. By growing wildflowers in your garden, you can contribute to their continuing survival and that of the wild creatures that depend upon them.

Index by English Name

English Name	Latin Name	Plant	Photo
Bird's Foot Trefoil	*Lotus corniculatus*	13	11
Bluebell	*Scilla non-scripta*	19	18
Cornflower	*Centaurea cyanus*	41	39
Cowslip	*Primula veris*	26	25
Field Scabious	*Knautia arvensis*	27	25
Foxglove	*Digitalis purpurea*	21	18
Great Mullein	*Verbascum thapsus*	41	39
Greater Knapweed	*Centaurea scabiosa*	29	25
Hoary plantain	*Plantago media*	27	25
Lady's Smock	*Cardamine pratensis*	33	32
Marsh Marigold	*Caltha palustris*	36	36
Meadow Cranesbill	*Geranium pratense*	28	25
Moon Daisy	*Leucanthemum vulgare*	26	25
Musk Mallow	*Malva moschata*	42	39
Pasque Flower	*Pulsatilla vulgaris*	12	11
Perennial Flax	*Linum perenne*	12	11
Primrose	*Primula vulgaris*	21	22
Purple Loosestrife	*Lythrum salicaria*	35	32
Ragged Robin	*Lychnis flos-cuculi*	34	32
Red Campion	*Silene dioica*	19	18
Sea Campion	*Silene uniflora*	14	11
Small Scabious	*Scabiosa columbaria*	13	11
Snake's Head Fritillary	*Fritillaria meleagris*	34	32
Stinking Hellebore	*Helleborus foetidus*	20	18
Sweet Violet	*Viola odorata*	20	18
Teasel	*Dipsacus fullonum*	43	39
Viper's Bugloss	*Echium vulgare*	40	39
Water Mint	*Mentha aquatica*	33	32
Wild Marjoram	*Origanum vulgare*	40	39
Yellow Stonecrop	*Sedum acre*	14	15

Index by Latin Name

Suppliers of Native Wildflower Seeds

Wildflower Seed.
Emorsgate Seeds, Limes Farm, Tilney All Saints, Kings Lynn, Norfolk. PE34 4RT.
Telephone: 01553 829028.

Suffolk Herbs.
Monks Farm, Coggeshall Road, Kelvedon, Colchester, Essex CO5 9PG
Telephone: 01376 572456

Suppliers of Wildflower Plants

Naturescape
Wildflower Farm, Lapwing Meadows, Coachgap Lane, Langar, Nottingham
NG13 9HP
Telephone: 01949 860592

Landlife Wildflowers
National Wildflower Centre, Court Hey Park, Liverpool L16 3NA
Telephone: 0151 7371819

Flower Farms
Carvers Hill Farm, Shalbourne, Marlborough, Wiltshire. SN8 3PS
Telephone: 01672 870782.

John Shipton
Y Felin, Henlann Amgoed, Whitland, Carmarthenshire. SA34 0SL
Telephone: 01994 240125
www.bluebellbulbs.co.uk

Further Reading

Creating a Wildlife Garden.
Bob and Liz Gibbons. (Hamlyn Books, 1988), 157pp.
[An excellent general book with good ideas, information and photographs, plus some garden designs for small or large gardens.]

How to Make a Wildlife Garden.
Chris Baines. (Francis Lincoln Ltd, 2000), 192pp.
[A good all round book, updated in 2000 from the original book published in 1985.]

The National Trust Book of Wildflower Gardening.
John Stevens. (Dorling Kindersley 1987), 192pp
[The definitive book on wildflower gardening, now out of print, but worth searching for.]

The Red Mason Bee: Taking the Sting out of Beekeeping.
Christopher O'Toole. (*Osmia* Publications, 2000), 34pp
[A practical guide to managing *Osmia rufa* as a pollinator in gardens, allotments and orchards.]

Wild Flower Gardening.
Michael Jefferson-Brown. (Cassell 1990), 64pp.
[One in the Wisley Handbook Series from The Royal Horticultural Society with good accurate information.]